Warm Holiday Wishes

Gail Sattler

When wise men saw the star at night
Shining to the world with Holy light
They traveled far to see the boy
Who soon would fill all hearts with joy.

At this time every year
Come love and wishes we
all hold dear;
And now without much
further ado
This book is full of wishes for you!

"For God so loved the world
that he gave his one
and only Son,
that whoever believes in
him shall not perish
but have eternal life."

John 3:16

Wishing You Peace, Joy, and Love

"Happy Holidays!"

—A QUOTE FROM YOUR FRIENDLY NEIGHBOR

May you be filled with peace
as the holiday season brings forth
the celebration of the birth of
our Lord Jesus Christ!

Look, there on the mountains,
the feet of one who brings good news,
who proclaims peace!

NAHUM 1:15

Each wish for the joy of the season
draws us closer together
at this happy holiday time.

Sing for joy, O heavens, for the LORD has done this;
shout aloud, O earth beneath. Burst into song, you
mountains, you forests and all your trees, for the LORD
has redeemed Jacob, he displays his glory in Israel.

ISAIAH 44:23

May you be filled with love
this holiday season, and
may it remain to bless you
every day throughout the coming year.

DO EVERYTHING IN LOVE.

1 CORINTHIANS 16:14

My Wishes for You

"Forget the shopping
and let's go have some hot chocolate."

—A QUOTE FROM YOUR BEST FRIEND

I WISH YOU MANY BLESSINGS
AS CHRISTMASTIME DRAWS NEAR.
MAY EVERYTHING THE HOLIDAYS HAVE TO OFFER
COME TO YOU THIS YEAR!

Grace and peace to you
from God our Father
and the Lord Jesus Christ.

1 CORINTHIANS 1:3

My deepest wishes for you are:
A joyful soul, a happy heart,
and wondrous eyes that see the miracles
within and around you.
May you be richly blessed
this Christmas season
and through all the days to come!

"As the Father has loved me,
so have I loved you.
Now remain in my love."

John 15:9

*Wishing you the happiest of holidays and a heart full
of joy in this Christmas season and coming New Year!*

May this beautiful season abound
and fill you with happy memories,
pleasant todays,
and joyful tomorrows.

AND SO WE KNOW AND RELY ON
THE LOVE GOD HAS FOR US.
1 JOHN 4:16

Christmas Is a Time of Joy

"Joy to the world, the Lord has come!"

—A QUOTE FROM THE
NEIGHBORHOOD CHRISTMAS CAROL GROUP

May the meaning of Christmas be deeper,
its friendships stronger,
and its hopes brighter
as it comes to you this year.

HOW GREAT IS THE LOVE
THE FATHER HAS LAVISHED ON US,
THAT WE SHOULD BE CALLED CHILDREN OF GOD!

1 JOHN 3:1

Christmas bells are ringing
All across the earth
Asking for God's blessings,
And proclaiming Jesus' birth.

NORMAN P. LUKER

O come, let us sing unto the Lord:
let us make a joyful noise
to the rock of our salvation.

PSALM 95:1 KJV

The angels sang their carols
And the bright star lit the way
To tell the world that Christ was born
That first glad Christmas day.

EDYTHE H. OULLIBER

HE SHALL BE GREAT,
AND SHALL BE CALLED
THE SON OF THE HIGHEST.

LUKE 1:32 KJV

All things bright and beautiful,
All creatures great and small,
All things wise and wonderful:
The Lord God made them all.

Cecil Alexander

For unto us a child is born,
unto us a son is given.

Isaiah 9:6 KJV

Sing a song, the Lord is born,
Shout for joy today!
The angels proclaim His glorious birth,
God's word they will obey.

From near and far, to rich and poor
Their songs resound with joy.
The world will hear the angels' shouts
Proclaiming Mary's baby boy.

GAIL SATTLER

Glory to God
in the highest.

LUKE 2:14 KJV

FOR OUR HEART SHALL REJOICE IN HIM,
BECAUSE WE HAVE TRUSTED
IN HIS HOLY NAME.

PSALM 33:21 KJV

God said,
"Jesus Is Coming!"

"Christmas is in ten sleeps!"

—A QUOTE FROM THE CHILD NEXT DOOR

For to us a child is born, to us a son is given, and the government will be on his shoulders. And he will be called Wonderful Counselor, Mighty God, Everlasting Father, Prince of Peace. Of the increase of his government and peace there will be no end. He will reign on David's throne and over his kingdom, establishing and upholding it with justice and righteousness from that time on and forever. The zeal of the LORD Almighty will accomplish this.

ISAIAH 9:6–7

The Messiah will be from David's family.

The Lord swore an oath to David,
a sure oath that he will not revoke:
"One of your own descendants
I will place on your throne."

PSALM 132:11

He will be born in Bethlehem.

"But you, Bethlehem Ephrathah,
though you are small among the clans of Judah,
out of you will come for me
one who will be ruler over Israel,
whose origins are from of old,
from ancient times."

MICAH 5:2

He will go to Egypt.

"When Israel was a child, I loved him,
and out of Egypt I called my son."

Hosea 11:1

He will live in Galilee.

Nevertheless, there will be no more gloom
for those who were in distress.
In the past he humbled the land of Zebulun
and the land of Naphtali, but in the future
he will honor Galilee of the Gentiles,
by the way of the sea, along the Jordan.

Isaiah 9:1

OTHERS WILL PROUDLY ANNOUNCE THAT
JESUS CHRIST IS COMING.

A voice of one calling: "In the desert prepare the way for the LORD; make straight in the wilderness a highway for our God."

ISAIAH 40:3

"See, I will send my messenger,
who will prepare the way before me.
Then suddenly the Lord you are seeking
will come to his temple;
the messenger of the covenant, whom you desire,
will come," says the LORD Almighty.

MALACHI 3:1

For he received honor and glory
from God the Father
when the voice came to him
from the Majestic Glory, saying,
"This is my Son, whom I love;
with him I am well pleased."

2 PETER 1:17

Jesus will love everyone.

"Here is my servant, whom I uphold,
my chosen one in whom I delight;
I will put my Spirit on him
and he will bring justice to the nations.
He will not shout or cry out,
or raise his voice in the streets.
A bruised reed he will not break,
and a smoldering wick he will not snuff out.
In faithfulness he will bring forth justice;
he will not falter or be discouraged
till he establishes justice on earth.
In his law the islands will put their hope."

ISAIAH 42:1–4

Peace and Joy
in the
Quiet Times

"When you're quiet,
you can hear the words."

—A QUOTE FROM THE NICE LIBRARIAN

When candles light
December nights
And Christmas joy unfolds,
Bright dreams abound
As peace surrounds
The gifts this season holds.

So gather 'round
And hear the sound
Of singing 'round the earth.
The heavens ring
When we all sing
Proclaiming Jesus' birth.

My Special Prayer for You

You are special to me and special to Jesus. He came to earth on Christmas Day because He loves you. I pray that your days during this holiday season will be as special and unique as you are. I pray that the peace and joy of Christmas will abide with you throughout the year.

May all the days of this Christmas season be filled with joy and happiness, and may the spirit of the season stay in your heart always.

May God touch you and keep you and your loved ones safe and happy and satisfied with His great love for the whole Christmas season and in all the days to come.

I pray that the love of Christ, whose birth we celebrate, will bless you and those you love with peace and joy forevermore.

Most of all, I pray that the presence of Jesus will fill your heart and home with everlasting joy.

May Peace and Beauty, Hope and Love
Be with you through the year;
May the love of friends and family
Bring you lots of cheer.

May everlasting Joy and Faith
Always fill your heart with praise;
May the wondrous holiday season
Bless you all your days.